Sieur de la Salle

Sieur de la Salle

Don Nardo

Franklin Watts
A Division of Scholastic Inc.
New York • Toronto • London • Auckland • Sydney
Mexico City • New Delhi • Hong Kong
Danbury, Connecticut

Note to readers: Definitions for words in **bold** can be found in the Glossary at the back of this book.

Photographs ©: Art Resource, NY: 34, 35 (Giraudon); Bridgeman Art Library International Ltd., London/New York: 24 (BAL108936/Private Collection); Buddy Mays/Travel Stock: 47; Canadian Heritage Gallery: 11 (C-6031/After P.L. Morin/National Archives of Canada) Canadian Heritage Gallery: 20 (C-47435/National Archives of Canada) Canadian Heritage Gallery: 19 (C-13325/J.H. de Rinzy/National Archives of Canada) Canadian Heritage Gallery: 51 (POS-5499/National Archives of Canada with permission of Canada Post Corporation) Chicago Historical Society: 2; Corbis-Bettmann 44 (Buddy Mays), 10, 40; James P. Rowan: 26, 30, 31, 39; Mary Evans Picture Library: 28 (Macpherson Collection), 42; North Wind Picture Archives: 5 top, 13, 33, 46, 50; Stock Montage, Inc.: 36; Stone: 43 (Nathan Benn), Stone: 14,15 (Ryan Beyer); Superstock, Inc.: 8 (Christie's, London), 16; Texas Historical Commision: 49; The Art Archive: 5 bottom, 18 (Musee des Arts Africains et oceaniens/Dagli Orti), 9 (Dagli Orti), 22 (Musee de Versailles/Dagli Orti).

Map by XNR Productions

Cover illustration by Stephen Marchesi

The illustration on the cover shows the French explorer René-Robert Cavelier, Sieur de la Salle. The photograph opposite the title page shows La Salle as a young man.

Library of Congress Cataloging-in-Publication Data

Nardo, Don, 1947–
    Sieur de la Salle / by Don Nardo
        p. cm. — (Watts Library)
    Includes bibliographical references (p.) and index.
    ISBN 0-531-11973-4 (lib. bdg.)   0-531-16581-7 (pbk.)
    1. La Salle, Robert Cavelier, Sieur de, 1643–1687—Juvenile literature. 2. Explorers—North America—Biography—Juvenile literature. 3. Explorers—France—Biography—Juvenile literature. 4. Mississippi River Valley—Discovery and exploration—French—Juvenile literature. 5. Mississippi River Valley—History—To 1803—Juvenile literature. [1. La Salle, Robert Cavelier, sieur de, 1643–1687. 2. Explorers. 3. Mississippi River—Discovery and exploration.] I. Title. II. Series.
F1030.5 N37   2001
977'.01'092—dc21
[B]
                                                                                                          00-049984

Contents

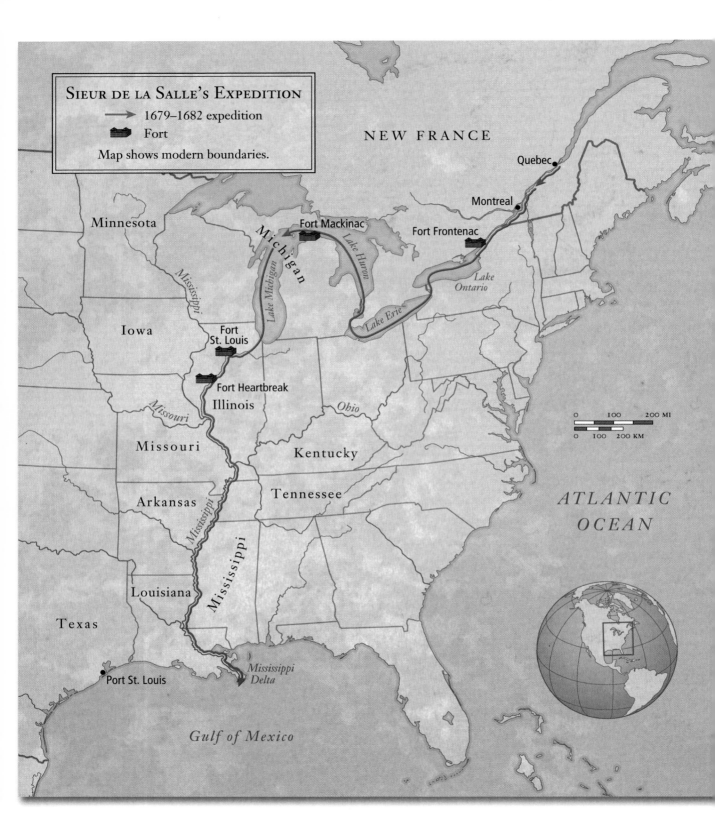

NEW FRANCE

Quebec

Montreal

Fort Frontenac

Fort Mackinac

Lake Huron

Lake Ontario

Lake Erie

Michigan

Lake Michigan

Minnesota

Mississippi

Iowa

Fort St. Louis

Fort Heartbreak

Illinois

Missouri

Ohio

Kentucky

Missouri

Arkansas

Tennessee

Mississippi

Louisiana

Mississippi

Texas

Port St. Louis

Mississippi Delta

Gulf of Mexico

ATLANTIC OCEAN

0   100   200 MI

0   100   200 KM

Chapter One

A Man With Big Dreams

Few European explorers dreamed on as grand a scale as René-Robert Cavelier, Sieur de la Salle. In the late 1600s, he boldly set out to create for his native France a North American empire, a vast new realm consisting of much of what is now the United States. He pictured this new empire stretching from the wilds of southern Canada, southward past the Great Lakes, through then largely uncharted lands of the American Midwest, and still further southward to the sandy shores of Louisiana along the Gulf of Mexico. Had he succeeded, the history of North America, and perhaps of the entire world, would have been very different.

In the end, however, bad luck and betrayal kept La Salle from accomplishing his dream. Nevertheless, he became the first European to travel down the Mississippi River to the Gulf of Mexico. And his daring expeditions opened up the Mississippi Valley and the American Midwest to European settlement.

The Young Jesuit

La Salle was born on November 21, 1643, in Rouen, a French city about 70 miles (113 kilometers) northwest of Paris. His real name was Robert Cavelier. He was the second son of Jean Cavelier, a successful local merchant, and his wife Catherine. To his family's surprise, young Robert developed an urge to travel to strange, faraway lands early on. At first, he intended

This painting depicts Rouen, the town where Robert was born.

The Jesuits

The Society of Jesus, whose members are known as Jesuits, is a religious order of men established in Paris in 1534. Its founder, Saint Ignatius of Loyola, placed the order under the direct authority of the pope, the head of the Roman Catholic Church. By the time Ignatius died in 1556, the order had more than a thousand Jesuits. And it continued to grow rapidly in the century that followed. Today, the Jesuits are noted for their fine schools, including Georgetown and Fordham Universities, both in the United States.

to become a **missionary**, a person who travels to other places to convert people to the Christian faith. At age nine, his father enrolled him in a local grammar school run by an order of Catholic priests called the Jesuits. For almost a century, the Jesuits had been sending missionaries to distant lands, such as China, in the Far East, and North America, where France and other European nations had colonies.

Robert studied hard at a series of Jesuit schools and graduated with honors when he was about twenty years old. At that time, graduates often taught for a few years before becoming

New France

The North American territories claimed by France in the late 1500s and early 1600s were collectively called New France. They included much of southeastern Canada, the Great Lakes, and the Ohio Valley, situated directly south of those lakes.

priests and beginning their missionary work. Robert dutifully took a teaching position at a French grammar school, but he was restless and eager to start his missionary work. He wrote a letter to the Superior General of the Jesuits, saying: "I have been **petitioning** with the greatest eagerness for admission to China. . . . So now, as I have reached my twenty-third year . . . I most humbly plead [to be sent to China]."

Along with his newfound success as a landlord, La Salle thought it was important to have a noble-sounding name.

Journey to New France

When the Jesuits did not respond to his request, Robert decided to leave the order. However, instead of becoming a poor missionary in China, he decided instead to go to North America. He wanted to make himself a fortune and become famous. Luckily, his older brother, Jean, was already well established in the colony of New France, in what is now southeastern Canada. Jean, who belonged to an order of priests known as the Sulpicians, welcomed Robert when he arrived in Montreal

10

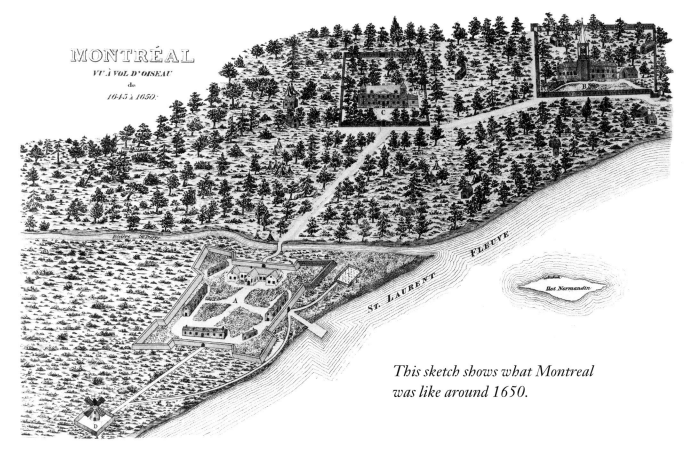

This sketch shows what Montreal was like around 1650.

in 1666. To help Robert fulfill his dream, the Sulpicians generously gave him a large, heavily forested piece of land in the area.

Robert was thrilled and thankful to receive his new property and immediately recruited settlers from France to live and work on it. It seemed to him that one thing was missing, though. Now that he was a respectable landlord, he should have an equally respectable name. He knew that nobles were the most respected members of French society. They enjoyed many more social privileges and advantages than ordinary people. To make himself sound more like a French nobleman, he adopted the title "de La Salle" ("of La Salle"), taking the name from a tract of family property called La Salle, near Rouen. As he had hoped, before long most people began calling him La Salle.

Eager and hardworking as always, La Salle soon developed his property, adding a fort and a successful trading post. But once again, he became restless and wanted more. In particular, he wanted to find out what lay beyond the horizon to the west and south. One day he heard some American Indians talking about a great river that flowed through the vast lands stretching south of the Great Lakes, in a region called Ohio. La Salle wondered if this river led westward to the Pacific Ocean. If so, it would be a **navigable** route to China, India, and other parts of the Far East.

Quest for a Northwest Passage

The idea of reaching the Far East by traveling west was not new. The famous Italian explorer Christopher Columbus was searching for such a westward route when he landed on an island in the Caribbean in 1492. As the years went by, other explorers remained convinced that a so-called Northwest Passage ran through North America to the Pacific Ocean. The race to find this legendary waterway continued because the stakes were so high. The man who discovered the Northwest Passage would open up valuable trade routes and make both himself and his country fabulously rich.

A Spaniard Finds the Mississippi

La Salle did not know that the Mississippi had already been seen by a European. In 1541, just over a century before La Salle was born, a Spanish explorer named Hernando De Soto stumbled on the great river. However, he explored only its lower reaches in what is now the state of Mississippi. People in La Salle's day had no idea that the river De Soto saw emptying into the Gulf of Mexico and the river described by the Great Lakes tribes were one and the same. So La Salle continued to hope that the legendary Mississippi or Ohio flowed westward into the Pacific Ocean.

La Salle believed that he could create a North American empire for France.

La Salle talked to other residents of New France about rivers in the wilderness to the south. He learned that European settlers in the Great Lakes region had long heard Indian tales about a mighty river called the Mississippi, running through the interior of the continent. La Salle had no way of knowing if the Ohio and Mississippi were two separate rivers or just different names for the same river.

Anxious to find these rivers—and the Northwest Passage—La Salle organized a small expedition. He and a few priests set out into the Ohio Valley wilderness in 1669. There is no evidence to prove whether he found the Ohio River on this trip. Some historians think he did. Others suggest that he spent most of 1669 and 1670 trading with the American Indians in the area, learning their languages, and becoming a skilled woodsman.

What is much more certain is that La Salle emerged from the wilderness with an even bigger dream than the one he had when he had entered it. He still wanted to find the Mississippi and the Northwest Passage. But now, he envisioned a huge French empire covering most of the continent. And he was convinced that fate had chosen him to become the founder of that mighty realm.

La Salle saw riches in the uncharted wilderness of North America.

Chapter Two

Master of Fort Frontenac

Like other European explorers before him, La Salle realized that the American wilderness could be a source of great wealth. That wilderness consisted in part of vast stretches of deep forests with cold, clear streams and lovely waterfalls. Large numbers of beavers and other animals made their homes in these woods and waterways, so there were valuable furs to be trapped. The wilderness also featured **formidable**, or large and imposing, mountains with a wide variety of rock

Overhunting the Beavers

The beavers that the French and other Europeans were so eager to trap for their elegant brown fur were generally about 4 feet (1.2 meters) long and weighed as much as 70 pounds (32 kilograms) when full grown. After La Salle's time, the trappers eventually overhunted these creatures, making them very scarce in the American Midwest. Only in modern times have beavers in the region increased in numbers and returned to their original habitats.

formations and minerals. Perhaps, therefore, as De Soto, Coronado, and other Spanish searchers had hoped, gold and other riches might be found.

To La Salle, creating a new French colony was more important than finding gold or other treasures.

But La Salle saw an even greater potential in these lands. What made him stand out from the other explorers was his daring dream of carving a huge new empire for France in the center of North America. He saw it encompassing Canada in the north, the Great Lakes, the unknown lands stretching southward to the Gulf of Mexico, and the lands lying farther west, leading to the Pacific coast.

La Salle realized that the key to securing the empire in North America he dreamed of was the fabled great river—the Mississippi. He was eager to find, chart, and claim such a long and navigable waterway for France. This would allow the French to ship people and goods far inland relatively easily and inexpensively. The

18

alternative was overland travel, which was far more time-consuming, dangerous, and expensive. By controlling the Mississippi, the French would be able to build forts, farms, and cities fairly quickly, giving them a strong foothold in the area. In addition, they would beat the Spanish, English, and other Europeans in the race for control of North America.

La Salle Meets Frontenac

The problem was that La Salle's dream was too big for most people. Most French settlers just wanted to work their farms or trade furs with the American Indians. Many, including most of the leaders of New France, thought La Salle's vision of massive expansion and development was too impractical and difficult to carry out.

Fortunately, one man believed in La Salle and his bold goal. After Louis de Buade, Count of Frontenac, became

This picture shows Louis de Buade, Count of Frontenac, who became governor of New France in 1672.

The Iroquois Confederacy

In La Salle's day, the Iroquois consisted of a group of five tribes— the Mohawk, Oneida, Onondaga, Cayuga, and Seneca. They were united in a **confederacy**, or partnership, which had a senate-like council in which representatives of each tribe voted on issues.

governor of New France in 1672, he and La Salle became friends. Frontenac saw qualities in La Salle that he believed he himself possessed, such as keen intelligence, courage, and intense curiosity about the unknown. One of La Salle's later colleagues, Henri Joutel, described the explorer as "large of soul, learned, designing, bold, **undaunted**, not to be discouraged at anything" and "wonderfully steady in **adversity**."

La Salle demonstrated his adventurous spirit early in his friendship with Frontenac. In 1673, he helped organize an important meeting between Governor Frontenac and the chiefs of the Iroquois Confederacy, a group of American Indian tribes inhabiting the Great Lakes region.

In a grand, colorful ceremony, the Iroquois signed a treaty, giving the French permission to build a fort on the northeastern shore of Lake Ontario. La Salle saw that facility, which was named Fort Frontenac in the governor's honor, as the first step in building the empire he dreamed of. The fort would be a starting point for French explorers and settlers heading into the wilderness.

Journey to France

Before any exploration and settlement could begin, however, La Salle and Frontenac had to solve a difficult problem. The governor had built the fort with his own money, expecting that the French royal government would pay him back. But Jean-Baptiste Colbert, King Louis XIV's minister of finance, refused. Seeing an opportunity to help both Frontenac and himself, La Salle journeyed to France in November 1674. There, he met and greatly impressed Colbert, who agreed to two major requests. First, Colbert used his influence with the king to make La Salle a noble. Making a commoner into a noble was not done very often and was considered to be a

The Sun King

Louis XIV ruled France from 1643 to 1715, the longest royal reign in European history. Known as the "Sun King," he supported scientific, artistic, and creative people in their pursuits.

great honor. The explorer happily became René-Robert Cavelier, Sieur de la Salle, sure that this title would open many doors for him.

Second, Colbert agreed that La Salle should become the owner of Fort Frontenac. "For the erection and establishment there of settlements," his **commission** read, "La Salle offers to **reimburse** the sum of ten thousand *livres*, the amount expended for the construction of said Fort Frontenac [and] to keep in good order the said fort." It was a good deal for all involved. The government would now pay back Count Frontenac. La Salle would pay back the government with the money he would make running the fort and its trading post. And La Salle, as master of Fort Frontenac, could become a very rich and influential man in New France.

The King Approves an Expedition

La Salle returned to New France in September 1675. He repaired and expanded Fort Frontenac and began trading over large parts of the surrounding region. The profits proved enormous, as he had expected. But once more, he began looking beyond, for he still intended to explore the center of the continent and build a French empire there.

With this goal in mind, in September 1677 La Salle made another trip to France, this time to ask for the king's permission to search for and explore the Mississippi. The region

An Eyewitness Describes the Fort

One of La Salle's colleagues, a man known simply as Minet, wrote a journal. In the journal he described Fort Frontenac as "a square of fifty **fathoms** [about 300 feet, or 90 meters] per side, three-quarters made of **masonry** [stone], three feet [1 m] thick and 12 to 16 feet [4 to 5 m] high, and the rest of posts. Inside there is a very handsome warehouse 20 by 25 fathoms [120 by 150 feet, or 36 by 45 m] in length, a guardhouse, a blacksmith shop, a house for the officers, a well, and another enclosed part that serves as a barnyard. There is a moat 20 feet [6 m] wide all around."

La Salle petitions the king for permission to explore the Mississippi River.

lying south and west of the Great Lakes, he told Colbert and the king, was "beautiful and fertile." It was "so abounding in fish, game, and **venison** [deer meat], that one can find there in plenty . . . all that is needful for the support of flourishing colonies." The soil, he continued, "will produce everything that is raised in France. . . . So there can be no doubt that colonies planted there would become very prosperous."

La Salle made such a strong case that the king granted his request. Using this royal commission to obtain credit, the delighted explorer managed to raise the money he needed for an expedition. And in July 1678, he set sail for New France with Henri de Tonti, a French naval officer who soon became his best friend and most trusted colleague. At that moment, they could never have guessed what a difficult and dangerous adventure lay ahead of them.

In 1679, La Salle and Tonti reached the Niagara River.

Chapter Three

The Mississippi at Last

La Salle and Tonti knew that the fastest and easiest way to travel through the wilderness was by boat. So they planned to save much time and effort by taking advantage of the Great Lakes and the rivers flowing into them. In the winter of 1678 and spring of 1679, they arrived at the Niagara River, just above the now famous Niagara Falls. As it approaches

The Straits of Mackinac

Lakes Huron and Michigan are connected to each other by the Straits of Mackinac, a channel 4 miles (6 km) wide and 30 miles (48 km) long.

the falls, the normally calm river becomes a mass of **rapids,** swift-moving currents of choppy water topped by whitecaps. Tonti built a modest wooden ship with two white sails and five small brass cannons. La Salle named the ship the *Griffin* to honor Frontenac, whose family coat of arms displayed the likeness of a griffin—an imaginary creature part-lion and part-eagle.

The *Griffin* set sail in August 1679. It passed through Lake Erie, then turned north and **traversed** the length of Lake Huron until it reached Mackinac. This settlement located at the junction of Lakes Huron and Michigan was the main trading post of the northern lakes region.

Tonti built La Salle's ship, the Griffin, *and hoped to use it to meet up with La Salle on the southern shore of Lake Michigan.*

La Salle's plan was to leave Tonti in Mackinac to gather more men and supplies. La Salle himself would sail south to Green Bay, load up the *Griffin* with furs, and send it back to the Niagara. After unloading its cargo, the ship would return to Mackinac to pick up Tonti and his party. Meanwhile, La Salle and fourteen men would paddle canoes from Green Bay to the southern shore of Lake Michigan, where they would eventually meet Tonti and his party. The search for the Mississippi would then begin.

Fort Heartbreak

Unfortunately for La Salle, things did not go exactly as planned. First, the *Griffin* disappeared, never to be seen again. This forced Tonti to make the journey southward in canoes, as La Salle and his men had. Both parties faced severe difficulties along the way. First, they ran out of food and were not able to find much game in the woods, so they became extremely hungry. They nearly froze to death, encountering severe cold weather, snowstorms, and ice-choked streams. La Salle and Tonti counted themselves lucky that they found each other alive and well.

Reunited, the members of the expedition continued their trek. Soon they reached the Illinois River, which flows into Lake Michigan from the southwest. After traveling south along the river for several days, La Salle and his men made friends with a group of Illinois Indians. With the permission of these Illinois people, the expedition built a small fort on a

After facing many challenges, La Salle and the members of his expedition reach the Illinois River.

high bluff overlooking the river and spent the winter there. La Salle named it Fort Heartbreak, perhaps because of the troubles the expedition had already encountered.

By March 1680, it was obvious to La Salle that he lacked the kind of ship and the supplies he needed to go on. He decided to leave Tonti in charge of sixteen men at Fort

Heartbreak. Their orders were to build a ship that could navigate the rivers, hopefully including the Mississippi. La Salle took five men and headed back for New France to gather supplies. Describing the terrible journey, he later wrote: "The thaws of approaching spring greatly increased the difficulty of the way. . . . We [suffered] all the time from hunger; [slept] on open ground . . . [pushed] through thickets . . . sometimes wading whole days through marshes where the water was waist-deep."

The Rescue Mission

On Easter day in 1680, La Salle and his companions reached a French fort near Niagara Falls. Amazingly, they had covered more than 1,000 miles (1,610 km) of rugged wilderness on foot in just sixty-five days. La Salle soon received a discouraging letter from Tonti, however. Most of the men at Fort Heartbreak had mutinied, Tonti said, and wrecked and looted the fort. La Salle was troubled by this news and worried about his friend's safety.

La Salle immediately mounted a rescue mission, but when he reached Fort Heartbreak, his spirits sank. The fort was deserted and there was no sign of Tonti. Also, La Salle discovered many dead bodies in the nearby Indian villages, which lay in ruins. La Salle learned that the Iroquois had recently attacked the Illinois.

As usual, La Salle refused to be defeated. He struck out into the Ohio Valley, hoping to find Tonti. But at first, La Salle found only greater hardship. "Snow kept on falling for nineteen days in succession," he later said, "with cold so severe that I never knew so hard a winter."

Luckily, La Salle eventually found his friend Tonti, who told a hair-raising story of his recent adventures. When the war had erupted between the Iroquois and Illinois, he had been seriously wounded. Fortunately, though, an Iroquois chief had recognized Tonti as a Frenchman and treated his wound.

Descending the Great River

Tonti and La Salle led their small party back to Fort Frontenac. There, they mounted a fresh expedition. The new

party consisted of twenty-two Frenchmen, eighteen American Indian guides and hunters, and thirteen American Indian women and children. Departing in December 1681, they headed toward the southwest, intent on reaching and exploring the mighty Mississippi.

This time, there were no major mishaps in the Ohio Valley. Retracing the steps he had taken on his former journeys, La Salle led his party down the Illinois River. Finally, on February 6, 1682, they reached the junction of the Illinois and

On February 6, 1682, La Salle and his party found the Mississippi River.

The Father of Waters

The Indians called the Mississippi the "Father of Waters." From its source in Minnesota to its mouth on the Gulf of Mexico, the mighty river is 2,348 miles (3,779 km) long.

33

This painting shows La Salle's ships approaching Louisiana.

Mississippi Rivers. They were not the first Frenchmen to see the Mississippi—two other explorers, Jacques Marquette and Louis Joliet, had reached it a few years before. But Marquette and Joliet had not explored the river very far south. This La Salle intended to do.

The trip downriver took two months. On April 6, 1682, the expedition reached a fork, where the Mississippi divided into three channels. La Salle had a feeling that they were near the sea. He divided his party into three groups, each of which paddled down a channel. Sure enough, after traveling only a few miles, all three groups reached the river's mouth, where the Mississippi empties into the Gulf of Mexico.

Three days later, La Salle held a solemn ceremony on the shore, near what is now Venice, Louisiana. Proudly, he said, "In the name of King Louis XIV of France, I claim possession of this country of Louisiana, the seas, harbors, ports, bays, and all the nations, peoples, provinces, cities, mines, minerals, streams, and rivers, from this great river's mouth to its source." In a single stroke, La Salle had surpassed all the inland explorers who had come before him. He had made good on his promise and provided France with the foundation of a huge North American empire.

On the riverbank of the Mississippi, La Salle announced that the lands of the Mississippi belonged to France.

Chapter Four

A New Expedition

La Salle stood near the mouth of the Mississippi River. All around him were thick marshlands crisscrossed with shallow channels, their banks covered in dark mud and tall grass. He could hear the waves of the Gulf of Mexico breaking in the distance. Solemnly, he claimed the lands surrounding the river for France, fully realizing that this act made his future appear very bright. He hoped to make a quick, safe return journey to New France to announce his discoveries.

There he expected to be welcomed and praised for the great service he had done for his country.

Once more, however, events did not occur as La Salle had hoped and expected. On the way upriver, the party was attacked by an army of hostile American Indians. One of the Frenchmen later recalled: "All of a sudden we heard a loud shout all around us and at the same time a rain of arrows on us. We cried, 'To arms!'. . . The battle lasted until daybreak, with shooting constantly from one side or another." Luckily, La Salle and his people escaped with only minor injuries.

A Series of Misfortunes

When the expedition reached the Illinois River, La Salle became very ill. The cause of his illness is not known, but he may have had **malaria**, which causes high fever. Though he managed to recover, he lost forty days of valuable time.

When La Salle finally reached Mackinac in July 1682, he received several pieces of bad news. First, his old friend Frontenac had recently been replaced as governor of New France. The new governor, Joseph LeFebvre de La Barre, was

a weak old man who was being **manipulated**, or controlled, by La Salle's enemies. These were prominent citizens of the colony who were jealous of La Salle's connections with the governor and the king. They also envied his courage and leadership, qualities which most of them lacked. They wanted to see him become a penniless failure. Influenced by these men, La Barre said that La Salle was attempting to "build up an imaginary kingdom for himself." Claiming that La Salle had abandoned Fort Frontenac, the governor seized it and gave it to a French nobleman.

When La Salle reached Mackinac, he learned that much had changed during his absence.

Losing the fort and its trading post was a serious blow to La Salle. He owed a large sum of money to his **creditors**—the people who had loaned him money for his expeditions. Without an income, he would be ruined. And then he would never be able to achieve his dream of a French empire in North America.

La Salle decided that the way to solve his problems was to build another trading center. In the winter of 1682–1683, he erected Fort St. Louis atop a steep hill overlooking the Illinois River, several miles upstream from Fort Heartbreak. He and Tonti trapped furs until spring. But when they sent the furs to

La Salle hoped that Fort St. Louis would solve his financial problems.

New France to pay back La Salle's creditors, the governor's men seized them. Even worse, La Barre sent a force of men to take control of Fort St. Louis.

Appeal to the King

Faced with complete ruin, La Salle saw only one way out—to go back to France and appeal directly to King Louis XIV. La Salle arrived back in France in December 1683. During his journey, he had hatched new plans for building a North American empire and he included them in the proposal he laid before the king. New France should not be the base of operations for building the empire, La Salle said. Rather, the king should authorize La Salle to establish a new French colony at the mouth of the Mississippi. From there, the French would be in striking distance of New Spain, the Spanish colony. Eventually, La Salle would lead an army to conquer New Spain, making France's holdings even larger.

King Louis was greatly impressed by La Salle's ideas. He said that he would allow La Salle "to command under Our authority, as well as in the country which will be subject anew to our **dominion** [empire] in North America . . . as well as among the French and Indians." Louis also sent a letter to La Barre in New France. The king ordered the governor to restore all of La Salle's forts and other property, which Tonti would manage while La Salle was in Louisiana.

La Salle was overjoyed. The king had not only approved his plans and granted his requests, but had also given him

New Spain

The Spanish colony of New Spain had been established in 1535. It consisted of Mexico, much of what is now the southwestern United States, and parts of Central America.

La Salle had high hopes for his new expedition.

more men and supplies than he had asked for. When the new expedition left France in July 1684, it consisted of four ships. These were *Le Joly*, *La Belle*, *L'Aimable*, and the *St. François*. The three hundred or so members of the expedition included La Salle's brother, Jean Cavelier; his nephew, Crevel de Moranget; a number of women and children to help populate the colony; several priests; and a soldier named Henri Joutel, who kept a journal of the venture.

New Troubles for La Salle

Unfortunately for the ambitious explorer, his joy was soon replaced by stress, sickness, and uncertainty. The first problem was that he and the captain of *Le Joly*, Sieur de Beaujeu, did not get along. Beaujeu thought La Salle was mean-spirited and mentally ill. "His distrust is incredible," Beaujeu later wrote to a friend. "If he sees one of his people speak to the rest, he suspects something, and is gruff with them. . . . There are very few people who do not think that his brain is touched." In fact, La Salle had never been very trusting of others. And his frequent sicknesses and misfortunes had made him nervous, suspicious, and irritable. So Beaujeu's criticisms were probably not completely unfair.

Disagreements with Beaujeu were only the beginning of La Salle's troubles though. He developed a terrible fever and had to spend over two months ashore regaining his strength. While he was recovering, the *St. François*, with its valuable stores of goods, was captured by Spanish pirates.

Finally, and worst of all, when the three remaining ships entered the Gulf of Mexico, they could not find the mouth of the Mississippi. At one point, Joutel and some of the others were sure there was a large river nearby. La Salle sent some men ashore to look for it but, as Joutel wrote, they "returned without having seen anything, because a fog happened to rise." Instead of waiting a day or two and trying again, La Salle decided to move on toward the west. At the time, he could not have foreseen that this was a fatal mistake.

La Salle and his expedition searched fruitlessly for the mouth of the Mississippi.

La Salle's ships wandered in the Gulf of Mexico after missing the mouth of the Mississippi.

Chapter Five

Tragic Final Years

As La Salle's ships drifted farther and farther west in the Gulf of Mexico, he had no way of knowing that his expedition was doomed. Modern historians have long debated why the party was unable to find the mouth of the Mississippi. Some suggest that many parts of the Gulf coast look more or less the same from 1 mile (1.6 km) out at sea—the average distance of La Salle's ships from the shore. So it would have been easy to miss the spot where the river empties into the gulf.

On February 20, La Salle gave up the search for the mouth of the Mississippi by sea, and decided to land his ships.

Others point out that sailors in those days still did not have a reliable method of determining **longitude**. This is the precise distance a traveler has moved either east or west of a given point on the Earth's surface. Even a small mistake in calculating longitude can take a ship many miles off course.

Whatever the reason for the error, the ill-fated party sailed 400 miles (644 km) too far west. Seeing that his people were exhausted and sick of the cramped conditions on the ships, La

Salle decided to go ashore. On February 20, 1685, the expedition arrived in what is now Matagorda Bay in southeastern Texas. His hope was to rest for a while and then try to find the Mississippi on foot.

Attack and Disease Take a Toll

La Salle's decision to leave the ships in the bay proved to be the worst mistake of his career. He and his followers found themselves in bleak, barren, desert country with no shelter and almost no food. Some dry grasses and a few cactuses were the only plants growing in the mounds of sand and dirt that stretched toward some almost treeless, rocky hills on the horizon. They had no clean drinking water either. Not surprisingly, several people each day came down with illnesses marked by fever and vomiting. To make matters worse, *L'Aimable* suddenly ran into some rocks in the bay and sank. Nearly all of its valuable cargo was lost, including sixty barrels of wine, four cannons, and most of the tools and medicine. There was also trouble with the American Indians in the area, mainly because of an inability to communicate clearly. Three of La Salle's men were killed when the native people attacked a group of Frenchmen who were foraging for food.

The expedition found themselves in a hostile Texas landscape.

La Salle tried to make the best of things, to keep his people busy and to raise their spirits. He encouraged them to plant crops and to build a small fort, which he named Fort St. Louis. But the crops did not grow well in the dry soil. And almost every day some of the colonists died of disease or **malnutrition**. In addition, the Indians continued to harass the settlers.

Misery, Despair, and Death

While La Salle worked on developing Fort St. Louis, Beaujeu sailed his ship, *Le Joly*, away from the bay. He may have intended to search for the Mississippi's mouth, but if so, he never found it and eventually went back to France. There, the authorities, who felt that La Salle's expedition had already cost too much, decided not to send a rescue mission. La Salle and his desperate colonists were now on their own and down to one ship, *La Belle*. But *La Belle* too was lost while exploring the coast east of the fort. This left everyone in the colony stranded, with no way to get home.

After the colony had endured many months of misery, despair, and death, La Salle decided that he must try to reach

New France and gather relief supplies. He made his first attempt in April 1686. But it failed when fourteen of his party of twenty-two, all of them men, died or deserted him. In January 1687, he tried again, this time taking along his brother Jean Cavelier, nephew Moranget, Joutel, and fourteen other men. The farewell at Fort St. Louis, in which the women, children, and the few remaining men were left behind, was sad and tearful. "We took our leaves with so much tenderness and sorrow," Joutel remembered, "as if we have all presaged [known] that we would never see each other any more."

These words unfortunately came true. Before even leaving Texas, the party met with disaster. Some of the men had hated La Salle for a long time because he had punished them for breaking some of his rules. La Salle always demanded and enforced strict discipline among his followers, and those who were lazy, selfish, or dishonest usually came to resent him. Three of these men now had a heated argument with Moranget, and they killed him

The wreck of La Belle *was found off the coast of Texas in 1995.*

La Salle was murdered by members of his expedition.

with an ax. Fearing the explorer's wrath, the mutineers decided that he too must die. On March 19, 1687, they ambushed the forty-four-year-old La Salle and shot him in the head, killing him instantly.

La Salle's Legacy

La Salle's brother Jean Cavelier, Joutel, and a few others managed to escape. They headed for the Illinois Valley where they met up with Tonti. They did not tell him that La Salle had been killed though, because Cavelier had decided that the king must be the first to hear the bad news. Several months later, when Tonti finally heard of his friend's death, he broke into tears and declared, "One of the greatest men of the age is dead."

King Louis XIV was sorry to hear that La Salle was dead, but he decided that sending a rescue mission to the Texas colony would be a further waste of precious French resources. As it turned out, such a mission would have been

Canada issued a postage stamp to commemorate the three hundredth anniversary of his expeditions.

a waste. The remaining members of La Salle's doomed colony had already died of disease or been killed by Indians.

Looking back on the explorer's life, one must agree with Tonti that La Salle was a great man. It is true that he made few discoveries and his last—and most ambitious—expedition ended in complete failure. But he was one of the few Europeans of his time who saw the real promise of North America.

Furthermore, La Salle left a great legacy. His chain of forts in the Illinois Valley and his claiming of the Mississippi Valley for France opened the way for the development of these areas. The French began colonizing Louisiana in 1714. They did not give up this huge territory, which stretched from the Gulf of Mexico to the Canadian border, until 1803. That was the year of the Louisiana Purchase, when France sold this vast area to the United States for $15 million. Had it not been for La Salle, this deal, and with it the westward expansion of the United States, might never have taken place.

Timeline

1541	Spanish explorer Hernando De Soto becomes the first European to see the Mississippi River.
1643	La Salle is born in Rouen, France; Louis XIV, the "Sun King," becomes ruler of France.
1666	La Salle travels to the French colony of New France, in what is now southern Canada.
1669	La Salle leads some Catholic priests in search of the Ohio River but does not find it.
1677	La Salle travels to France and receives permission from King Louis XIV to search for the Mississippi River.
1679	La Salle explores the Illinois River Valley.
1682	After numerous attempts, La Salle reaches the Mississippi and canoes down its length to the Gulf of Mexico. There he claims the river and all the lands bordering it for France.
1684–1685	Leading a new expedition, La Salle attempts to find the mouth of the Mississippi. But he fails to find it and lands his party on the coast of what is now southeastern Texas.
1687	La Salle is murdered by some of his own men while attempting to reach New France.
1803	In the Louisiana Purchase, France sells Louisiana, the huge territory first claimed by La Salle, to the United States.

Glossary

adversity—hard times

commission—a grant of authority or permission given by a ruler or governing body

confederacy—a union or partnership

creditor—a person from whom one has borrowed money

dominion—an empire or realm; the control of an empire or realm

fathom—a unit of length or depth equal to about 6 feet (1.8 meters)

lofty—grand

longitude—the position of a place measured in degrees east or west of an imaginary line that runs through Greenwich, England

malaria—a disease spread by mosquitoes. The symptoms are chills, high fever, and sweating. Malaria can be fatal.

malnutrition—lack of a proper diet

manipulate—to control or influence, usually in a devious way

masonry—stone or brick

missionary—a person who tries to convert others to his or her religious beliefs

navigable—allowing the passage of ships

petition—a request

rapids—fast-moving, choppy, and usually dangerous river waters

reimburse—to pay back

traverse—to travel across

undaunted—brave or courageous in the face of any and all hardships

venison—deer meat

To Find Out More

Books

Coulter, Tony. *La Salle and the Explorers of the Mississippi*. New York: Chelsea House, 1991.

George, Charles and Linda George. *Mississippi*. Danbury, CT: Children's Press, 1999.

Hintz, Martin. *Missouri*. Danbury, CT: Children's Press, 1999.

Jacobs, William J. *La Salle: A Life of Boundless Adventure*. Danbury, CT: Franklin Watts, 1994.

Mudd-Ruth, Maria. *The Mississippi River*. Tarrytown, NY: Benchmark Books, 2000.

Rogers, Barbara Radcliffe and Stillman D. Rogers. *Canada*. Danbury, CT: Children's Press, 2000.

Santella, Andrew. *Illinois*. Danbury, CT: Children's Press, 1998.

Waldman, Carl. *Atlas of the North American Indian*. New York: Facts On File, 1985.

Organizations and Online Sites

Canadian Heritage Gallery
http://www.canadianheritage.org
View paintings, drawings, and original documents from Canada's rich history, including La Salle and other explorers.

Fort St. Louis
http://www.dallasnews.com/texas_southwest/0907tsw111fort.htm
An online article from the *Dallas Morning News* discusses the beginning of the archaeological study of La Salle's Fort St. Louis in Texas.

Life of La Salle
http://www.thc.state.tx.us/belle/LaS.html
This website offers a general overview of La Salle's life and expeditions.

New France
http://www.agt.net/public/dgarneau/french.htm
Visitors to this website can learn more about the history of the French colony of New France and find links to related sites.

Raising *La Belle*

http://www.caller.com/newsarch/lasalle1.htm

This website features an article from the *Corpus Christi Caller-Times* newspaper on the wreck of La Salle's ship, *La Belle*. The site also provides a chronology of La Salle's life and expeditions.

Texas Historical Commission

http://www.thc.state.tx.us/

This organization is a state agency that works to preserve Texas's archaeological, architectural, and cultural landmarks, including La Salle's Fort St. Louis and the wreck of his ship *La Belle*. From its website, you can see pictures of the wreck of *La Belle* and learn more about the commission's La Salle Archaeology Project.

Virtual Museum of New France

http://www.vmnf.civilization.ca/somm-en.htm

This online museum provides a wealth of information on New France, and offers special online exhibits. It also includes a glossary, a chronology of historical events, maps, and links to other related sites.

A Note on Sources

Out of all the many European explorers who came to North America, La Salle has always been one of the most fascinating for me. Perhaps that is because of the sadness of his lost potential. He had such extraordinary courage, determination, and vision. Yet his end was so tragic. His exploits would make a wonderfully dramatic and moving film, if Hollywood would wake up and realize it!

In writing this book about La Salle, I first collected and read the main primary (original) and modern sources about him. Among the most important of the handful of primary sources available is a journal kept during his last expedition by Henri Joutel, a soldier who was one of its few survivors. Without Joutel's first-hand account, it would be difficult to piece together the main events of that ill-fated venture. Of the modern sources, one of the best is *La Salle and the Discovery of the Great West,* by Francis Parkman (1823–1893), one of the most distinguished of all American historians. Though some new information about La Salle has been found since this book first appeared, it remains essential reading on the subject. La Salle was one of Parkman's heroes and the historian wrote about him and his times in enthusiastic, often elegant prose. I highly recommend this and Parkman's other books about early North America.

—*Don Nardo*

Index

Numbers in *italics* indicate illustrations.

About the Author

Don Nardo is a historian and award-winning writer. Among his many books about the history of North America are *The North American Indian Wars*, a comprehensive summary of the white conquest of the Native American tribes in what is now the United States; *The Mexican-American War*, which exposes the complex background, dirty politics, and needless brutality of one of America's forgotten conflicts; *Braving the New World*, the inspiring saga of the first black slaves in colonial America; and *The Declaration of Independence*, a detailed overview of the history and legacy of that famous document. Mr. Nardo lives with his wife Christine in Massachusetts.